Mustard Cookbook

Mustard is more than a condiment - This cookbook will make you realize it and more!

BY: Ivy Hope

Copyright/License Page

Table of Contents

Introduction

Of course, you should still keep your favorite bottles of mustards in your fridge: yellow, Dijon, maybe honey, or spicy ones. Now, you can also plant your very own mustard. Let us proceed.

So, make sure you do choose a time of the year to plant your seeds after the last frost if you like in a colder area. Try to avoid planting during the hot summer season, so spring is the best season to create your mustard garden. So, get the mustard seeds from your local garden center and get ready. You should place the seeds about 1 inch or less apart and just barely covered by the soil. You should find in an area on your property that is partially sunny. If you are planting in healthy soil, you should not have to use fertilizer, but if you think your soil needs it, it cannot hurt. If you do not get enough natural rain, make sure you water the seeds; they should get a few inches of water a week. It can be the perfect chore for the little ones wanting to help in the garden.

You will start seeing the leaves growing within a few weeks to a month. I think the easiest way to harvest mustard eaves is to pick up the leaves. You can leave the plant in the grown, ready to grow some more. Then, it is time to make some mustard! Use the plant's seeds, water, vinegar, and the right spices. Do not worry; we suggest many amazing recipes in the next section.

However, do not worry, ladies and gentlemen, if you prefer to simply buy the mustard that already made and ready to use in dishes, go for it! We will leave it up to you and what fits your budget and your time schedule. We just want to propose you as many options as possible as always. So put your apron on, and let's get cooking.

All spices homemade mustard

We are starting this cookbook with a bang! This mustard recipe is bold and delicious. We are leaving a room, as always, for your own interpretation and additions. However, try to keep the proportions, so your mustard ends up being the right texture.

Ingredients:

- 1 cup white balsamic vinegar
- 1/4 cup brown mustard seeds
- 1 tsp. seas salt
- 1/2 tsp. turmeric
- ½ tsp. ground cinnamon
- 1/4 tsp. black pepper
- 1 Tbsp. water

Servings: 4 +

Preparation time: 12 hours+

Method:

In a mixing bowl, put the water, vinegar and mustard seeds.

Normally you should let the mixture soak for about 12 hours.

Place the mixture in the blender container when the soaking period is done.

Add the rest of the ingredients and blend.

Taste and adjust spices or consistence accordingly.

Place in a glass container for storage and refrigerate.

Herbs mustard for you

There is nothing like making a homemade mustard with fresh herbs. Get your scissors out and get chopping in your garden. You can vary the type of herbs you will use for this recipe.

Ingredients:

- 1 cup rice vinegar

- 1 tbsp. minced fresh parsley

- 1 tbsp. minced fresh chives

- 1 tbsp. minced fresh oregano

- 1 tsp sea salt

- 1 tbsp. brown mustard seeds

- 2 tbsp. dried mustard powder

Servings: 4+

Preparation time: 12 hours +

Method:

Just like in the first recipe, we will let the mustard seeds soak in the vinegar for about 12 hours.

I have tried both, to let them herbs soak in with it or add them on later.

I decoded that I like to do half and half.

So, I add half of the suggested herbs with the mustard seeds and vinegar and keep the rest to add to the blender mixture.

When the soaking period is over, add all the rest of the ingredients in the blender and activate.

You might want to add actually just a little yellow mustard to the mixture to smooth it out, since it is going to be filled with herbs and textures.

Taste and adjust the spices accordingly.

Place in the glass jar and refrigerate until ready to use.

Simple but strong honey mustard

Because regular mustard does not please everyone, we have to invent other variations of mustards. That is my thought process anyway. Honey is a winning ingredient. Adding honey to your favorite mustard or creating your own honey mustard recipe can be life-changing… for your next sandwich!

Ingredients:

- ¼ cup your favorite Dijon mustard

- ½ cup sour cream

- ½ cup honey

- 2 tbsp. white vinegar

- 1 tsp. salt

- 1 tsp. smoked paprika

Servings: 4+

Preparation time: 10 min

Method:

No soaking necessary this time!

You will simply place all the ingredients in a mixing bowl and combine until the texture is smooth and the taste perfect.

Refrigerate the final product until ready to use, preferably in a glass jar.

The best mustard salad dressing you will ever taste

The next step is to make your own salad dressing mustard-based. You can and will truly embrace a homemade vinaigrette, compared to a store-bought one. You will be praised by your loved ones or guests when you serve it, as we will add only the best of the best ingredients you can find.

Ingredients:

- 2 egg yolks

- 1 Tsp. minced garlic

- 2 Tbsp. Dijon mustard

- 3 Tbsp. white balsamic vinegar

- ¼-cup olive oil

- Salt, black pepper

Servings: 4+

Preparation time: 10 min

Method:

This recipe is very similar to making a Caesar salad dressing.

It uses most of the same ingredients.

I like to say that you can absolutely change up the type of mustard you use to create it, since you now have a variety of homemade one sin the refrigerator to choose from.

Create and recreate this recipe differently over and over again!

Chicken stew with delicious mustard sauce

Not only will you be amazed by the lovely yellowish color of the stew, but also by its taste. I enjoy cooking some chicken breasts; the white part of the chicken is my favorite. However, you can also choose other parts such as thighs or legs, and this stew would be delightful also.

Ingredients:

- 2 pounds your favorite chicken parts, my favorite is breast, so I use 4-6 boneless chicken breasts for this recipe

- 2 minced green onions

- 1 tbsp. minced garlic

- 1 tbsp. olive oil

- 2 cups chicken broth

- 1 cup sour cream

- 1 Tbsp. yellow mustard

- ¼ cup sliced black olives

- Salt, black pepper

- 1 tbsp. balsamic vinegar

- 1 Tbsp. Italian seasonings

Servings: 4

Preparation time: 90 min

Method:

Clean the chicken breasts carefully and cut in large pieces, set aside.

In a large saucepan, heat the olive oil and cook for 10 minutes the garlic, onions.

Add next the chicken pieces and cook for at least 10-12 minutes – flipping the chicken half way.

When the chicken is done, add the rest of the ingredients and stir all together.

Note that you can at this point transfer all the ingredients into a crockpot, turn on low heat and leave to cook all day while you are at work.

You can also leave it in the large saucepan, continue cooking on the stove burner for 45 minutes or so.

I usually serve this stew on a bed of rice.

Mustard, veggies, and cheese casserole

A Veggies and Cheese Casserole needs a little kick if not, it can become a very plain dish. Some add some hot sauce salsa, a lot of garlic, or spicy cheese. We will add some mustard and other key ingredients to make it as delicious as healthy.

Ingredients:

- 2 cups fresh cauliflower florets

- 2 cups fresh broccoli florets

- 6 cups vegetables broth, to cook veggies

- 1 cup sour cream

- 1 package plain cream cheese

- 2 cups shredded Cheddar cheese

- 1 tbsp. yellow mustard

- 1 tbsp. minced garlic

- 1 small chopped sweet onion

- 1 tsp. red pepper flakes

- Sea salt

- 1 tsp. ground cumin

Servings: 6-8

Preparation time: 55 min

Method:

Preheat the oven to 400 degrees F.

Grease a square or rectangle large dish and set aside.

Boil the vegetables broth and steam cook the broccoli and cauliflower for only 5 minutes.

Set aside and drain well.

In a small pan, heat some oil and cook the garlic and onions for about 5 minutes.

In a large mixing bowl. Combine the cream cheese, sour cream, mustard, salt, cumin and red pepper flakes.

Add the cooked veggies and stir all together.

Dump into the dish and spread evenly.

Add the Cheddar cheese on top, and place in the oven for 30 minutes.

Serve as a side dish or if you are vegetarian, as a main dish.

Tasty mustard and chicken bouillon

Have you ever been sick and strictly confine in eating chicken bouillon? Perhaps, you remember being bored after a few bowls. But this soup is tasty, and you will not even need to add noodles if you are looking for a gluten-free soup.

Ingredients:

- 8 cups chicken broth

- 1 tsp. Dijon mustard

- Salt, black pepper

- 1 Tbsp. soy sauce

- 1 minced leek

- 1 block firm tofu, well drained

- 1 tsp. minced garlic

- 1 tbsp. unsalted butter

- Bacon bites to decorate (optional)

Servings: 4

Preparation time: 40 min

Method:

In a large saucepan, heat the butter and cook the garlic and leek for 7-8 minutes.

Make sure to drain carefully the tofu and set aside.

Add the broth and all other ingredients, except the tofu and bacon.

Bring to boil and then lower to simmering temperature for 20 minutes.

For the last 10 minutes, add the tofu and bacon and serve in a large bowl, perhaps with fried rice noodles on top if you like.

Sausage in a skillet with an incredible mustard kick

I typically eat my hot dogs or any kind of sausage, in fact, with mustard. So, this dish makes total sense to me. This sauce and added ingredients marry perfectly with the sausages and make it look so appetizing!

Ingredients:

- 4 bratwursts of your choice (mild to medium)

- 1 sliced red bell pepper

- 1 sliced green bell pepper

- 1 small sliced yellow onion

- 1 tbsp. minced garlic

- 1 tbsp. olive oil

- ¼ cup vegetables broth

- 1 tbsp. Dijon mustard

- ¼ cup sour cream

- 1 tsp. hot sauce

- Salt, black pepper

Servings: 3-4

Preparation time: 45 min

Method:

You will need a large pan, preferably an iron cast one.

.In the pan, heat the oil and cook the garlic, onions, peppers together for 10 minutes. Set aside.

Cut the sausages in 4-6 pieces each and start cooking in the pan as well.

Stir often, and make sure the sausages are cooked all the way.

Remove the sausages when done for a moment.

In the pan, dump the sour cream, mustard, hot sauce, broth and spices.

Stir well and then add the sausages and veggies.

Let the ingredients simmer together for about 20 minutes.

Serve hot.

Try this lovely salmon and mustard recipe

This salmon will be baked and made with love and mustard. We do not want to use too much mustard or too strong of mustard, as the salmon as its own very taste we want to reserve. Therefore, measure your ingredients well and taste and adjust.

Ingredients:

- 4 salmon fillets

- 1 tsp. yellow mustard

- ¼ cup dry white wine

- 1 Tbsp. olive oil

- 2 Tbsp. sesame seeds

- ½ cup vegetables bouillon

- ½ cup heavy fresh cream

- 1 Tbsp. capers

Servings: 4-6

Preparation time: 45 min

Method:

Preheat the oven to 375 degrees F.

Grease a large rectangle dish and set aside.

.In a small saucepan, heat the sesame seeds in oil and add the wine, bouillon and mustard.

Add also the cream next and stir.

Season the salmon filets with salt and pepper on each side.

Place skin down on the dish and add the sauce on top as well as the capers.

Cook in the oven for 25-30 minutes.

Serve with lemon wedges.

Mustard and corn side dish

This recipe is so interesting! I love making this side dish with my Mexican or Cuban dishes. I also sometimes use it just to add color to a simple entrée, such as steak and potatoes. This yellow very appetizing dish makes any plate stick out and make you want to find out how does the mustard truly marry with corn!

Ingredients:

- 4 cups fresh kernel corn grains

- 1 Tbsp. homemade honey mustard

- 1 Tbsp. lime juice

- 1 tbsp. minced fresh chives

- 1 tbsp. minced fresh parsley

- Black pepper

- Pinch salt

- 1 Tbsp. avocado oil

- 1 large diced avocado, to decorate

Servings: 8-12

Preparation time: 50 min

Method:

If you choose to boil your corn on the cob and get the grains to make the recipe, more power to you!

I often use the organic canned corn and I love the taste and nutrients.

.Either way, combine in a large mixing bowl the avocado oil, salt, pepper, herbs, lime juice and mustard.

Then add the corn and combine well.

When ready to serve, peel and dice a fresh avocado and top off your corn dish with it.

This is a yummy side to any grilled meat or baked fish.

To make yummy devil eggs you need mustard

Let us boil the eggs, let us peel the eggs, and let us add some mustard. This recipe will also add some additional surprise ingredients that might leave some speechless but will certainly add proteins to your day.

Ingredients:

- 12 hardboiled eggs

- ½ cup mayonnaise

- ¼ cup sour cream

- 1 Tbsp. yellow mustard

- Salt, black pepper

- Smoked paprika

- ¼ cup crumbled bacon bites

Servings: 6+

Preparation time: 1 hour

Method:

Hard-boil your eggs as you normally do and remove the shells carefully.

Slice the eggs, once they have cooled down, lengthwise.

Remove the middle, the cooked yolk and place in a mixing bowl.

Place the while halves on a serving plate.

In the mixing bowl, add the mayonnaise, mustard, sour cream, spices and bacon.

Combine well and stuff all half eggs with this mixture you just created.

Refrigerate the eggs if you are not serving them right away.

Spicy mustard sautéed cauliflower

Cauliflower can be a pretty blend veggie. It should be seasoned with care and good taste. We will choose a spicy mustard here for this particular recipe. We will also add some garlic and other seasonings. If you absolutely can't stand cauliflower, try this recipe with squash!

Ingredients:

- 1 large cauliflower head, cut in florets

- 1 Tbsp. Dijon mustard

- ½ tsp. turmeric

- Pinch ground cinnamon

- 2 tbsp. unsalted butter

- 1 tbsp. Olive oil

- 3 tbsp. orange juice

- 1 tsp. red pepper flakes

Servings: 4

Preparation time: 30 min

Method:

Boil water in saucepan and steam cook the cauliflower.

Drain well and set aside.

In a large pan, heat the butter and add the juice, spices, mustard and stir well.

Then add the cauliflower.

Make sure the sauce covers all florets and keep cooking in the pan for another 10-12 minutes.

Serve warm as a side dish with any meat, poultry or fish.

Noodles, greens and mustard dish

We can make this dish just with greens and delicious butter noodles, or we can decide to add tuna as extra proteins. Either way, you will add mustard as indicated in the recipe and appreciate all the ingredients combined together. What I love about this recipe is that you can choose to eat it cold or warm.

Ingredients:

- 1 bag or package of egg noodles

- 2 large cans drained tuna

- 1 Tbsp. favorite homemade mustard

- 1 cup sour cream

- 2 cups cooked fresh green beans

- Salt, black pepper

- Pinch ground cumin

Servings: 4

Preparation time: 30 min

Method:

You can choose to cook the butter noodles in salt water or even some broth of your choice.

Drain the noodles well when done and set aside.

Meanwhile, steam cook also the green beans, after you have washed them carefully and trimmed them.

Once the beans are cooked, cut them in smaller pieces, place them in a large mixing bowl.

Add the spices, the mustard, the sour cream and combine.

Finally, add the tuna and noodle and combine all ingredients well together.

This pasta salad can be served warm or cold, your choice.

Stuffed eggs sandwich with lots of mustard and more

This lovely sandwich idea can be served for breakfast, lunch, snack, or dinner. It can be served anytime because it is really super healthy, and if you are like me, you like breakfast anytime of the day! Now, let's find out if you like mustard anytime of the day !

Ingredients:

- Sourdough bread, slices (8 will make 4 sandwiches)

- 8 eggs

- 2 cups sliced fresh buttons mushrooms

- 1 Tbsp. honey mustard

- 1 tbsp. minced fresh oregano

- Salt, pepper

- 1 Tbsp. unsalted butter

- 1 cup shredded Swiss cheese

Servings: 4

Preparation time: 20 min

Method:

Let's assume you all want to eat your sandwiches at the same time, let's prepare the eggs together.

In a large pan, heat the butter and sautéed the mushrooms, after seasoning with salt and pepper for 12 minutes.

In a bowl, whisk the eggs, cheese, mustard and oregano together.

Add to the pan and cook for 7-8 minutes or until the eggs are done.

Meanwhile toast the bread just right and get ready to assemble the delicious eggs' sandwiches.

Making potatoes salad: you need mustard

My mom and grandmother made potatoes salad in the same way. I modified their recipe over the years to accommodate my family's tastes. I changed many ingredients, including the type of potatoes I used, but one thing remains the same: yellow mustard is a key.

Ingredients:

- 2 pounds white potatoes, peeled

- 1 cup mayonnaise

- 1 tbsp. yellow mayonnaise

- Salt, black pepper

- 2 tbsp. dill relish

- 1 tsp. smoked paprika

- 3 tbsp. sliced black olives

Servings: 6-8

Preparation time: 50 min

Method:

Wash the potatoes and peel them. Boil water and salt in a large saucepan. Cut the potatoes in smaller pieces and cook for 12 minutes or so. You don't want to overcook the potatoes, as they should not be mushy.

When cooked, drain the potatoes well and set aside to cool down.

In a large mixing bowl, combine the mayonnaise, mustard, and all other ingredients.

Carefully add the potatoes and stir all together.

Make sure to refrigerate the potatoes salad if you are not ready to eat it right away.

Yummy shrimp in mustard sauce

This sauce or recipe overall will be surprised you on how easy it is to make! Get some fresh or frozen and thawed shrimp, the ingredients for the yummy sauce, and you are in business. I love serving the dish on rice noodles, but by default, you can also serve it on rice.

Ingredients:

- 1 pound shrimp, medium, deveined, peeled

- 1 small diced yellow onion

- 1 Tbsp. minced garlic

- 2 Tbsp. minced fresh cilantro

- 2 Tbsp. lime juice

- 1 tsp. red pepper flakes

- 1'2 tsp. sea salt

- 1 Tbsp. homemade spicy mustard

- 1 cup sour cream

- ½ cup vegetables bouillon

Servings: 4

Preparation time: 30 min

Method:

Line up all the ingredients on the kitchen counter.

In a large skillet, heat the olive oil and sautéed garlic, onions and cilantro for about 10 minutes on medium heat.

Add the shrimp and cook and other 12 minutes or until the shrimp change color to pink.

Add the rest of the ingredients and stir all the ingredients together and let them simmer for another 15 minutes.

Serve on a bed of rice noodles or cooked rice.

Yummy lemon and mustard rice

You will add yellow ingredients to this recipe, so you should definitely anticipate a yellow rice! Lemon juice and mustard will be added, along with other must-have ingredients. I enjoy serving this rice with skewers on top or maybe just grilled veggies displayed on this pretty yellow side dish.

Ingredients:

- 2 cups white rice of your choice

- 4 cups turkey or chicken bouillon

- 1 Tbsp. lemon juice

- 1 Tbsp. Dijon mustard

- 2 minced green onions

- 1 Tbsp. olive oil

- ½ tsp. turmeric

- Salt, pepper

Servings: 4

Preparation time: 30 min

Method:

Heat the broth in a large saucepan and add the rice to cook.

Cook according to the package instructions or as you normally would.

Drain the rice as needed. In a large skillet, heat olive oil, cook the green onions, and add all the other ingredients including the rice.

Sautéed the rice and stir often for about 10 minutes or until it turns nice and yellow.

Serve this beautiful rice with a white fish or chicken to add some color on your plate!

Scrumptious mustard and veggies fish stew

When you make a fish stew, you want to choose a fish that is not too flaky. I lie to use cod, so I can cut small but thick pieces, and I know they will stay whole when cooked and make it more interesting to eat. This stew is just fabulous and so healthy for you and your family. I have tricked my kids to think that it was chicken for the longest time, and now they eat it although they know it's fish!

Ingredients:

- 1 pound cod fillets

- 4 cups fresh baby spinach

- ½ cup diced red onion

- 1 Tbsp. minced garlic

- 1 tbsp. olive oil

- 4 cups vegetables broth

- ½ cup sherry wine

- 1 tbsp. yellow mustard

- 1 Tbsp. of your favorite homemade spicy mustard

- ½ tsp. cumin

- Salt, black pepper

Servings: 4-6

Preparation time: 55 min

Method:

Clean the fillet of fish nicely and season with salt and pepper on each side. Cut into 3-4 pieces each. Set aside for now.

Use a large saucepan and heat oil on medium temperature. Add the garlic, onions and cook for 6-7 minutes.

Add the sherry wine next and the fish.

Cook the fillets on each side for about 10 minutes or until done.

Then, add the rest of the ingredients. Make sure to stir well so all the flavors can mix.

Let the stew simmer for another 30 minutes or more.

Taste before serving and adjust seasonings as needed.

Superb whole wheat mustard, turkey and Swiss cheese sandwich

The bread, the meat cheese, and the mustard you will use for your sandwich matter. They all matter equally. If you want a certain taste, get used to utilizing the right quality ingredients. I think you will like what we propose here. I have used artichoke hearts or banana peppers sometimes in addition to the main ingredients to keep it fun and different. Create your own version!

Ingredients:

- 8 slices rye bread (or any other favorite)

- 4 thick slices Swiss or provolone cheese

- 8 slices smoked turkey

- 2 Tbsp. mayonnaise

- 1 tbsp. Dijon mustard

- 1 cup arugula lettuce

- 1 sliced large tomato

- Salt, black pepper

Servings: 4

Preparation time: 12 min

Method:

Nothing is complicated about this recipe, just simple ingredients for incredible taste!

Put your bread in the toaster if you want it toast and gather all the other ingredients on the kitchen counter.

Get ready to make sandwiches.

I like to combine the mayonnaise and mustard ahead in separate bowl and spread this mixture on the hot bread.

Add the lettuce, cheese, meat and tomatoes. Season the tomato with salt and pepper.

And here you go, you have a delicious sandwich ready for the family in no time.

Remember to use your footie mustard for this recipe!

Pork tenderloin or pork chops with awesome mustard sauce

Pork, as we all know, can be very dry, so to serve it with a sauce is, to begin with an excellent idea. To serve the pork with a mustard sauce is an extraordinary idea, and many of you will adopt this recipe when you want to make a pork dish. Enjoy every bite of it!

Ingredients:

- 4 boneless pork chops
- 1 Tbsp. unsalted butter
- 1 Tbsp. flour
- Salt, black pepper
- 1 Tbsp. Dijon mustard
- 2 cups heavy cream
- ½ cup turkey or chicken bouillon
- Pinch cumin
- Pinch nutmeg

Servings: 4-6

Preparation time: 40 min

Method:

Preheat oven at 375 degrees F.

Grease a large baking dish and set aside.

Season the pork chops on each side with salt and pepper.

In a large skillet, heat the butter and cook for only a few minutes on each side. It will not be fully done, but that is okay, it will finish cooking the oven.

In a medium saucepan, prepare the sauce.

Bring to boil the following: mustard, cumin, nutmeg, cream and flour.

Once it has thickened enough, reduce to low temperature.

Place the pork chops on the dish and pour sauce on top. Cover with foil paper to avoid the pork from getting dry.

Bake for about 20 minutes or so.

Garlic and mustard spiced sautéed shrimp

We will pick some ingredients that might surprise you, but, at the end, you will be enchanted! Stay tuned and please use the green onions; it will add that green touch needed. Enjoy this recipe with a glass of dry white wine if you like.

Ingredients:

- 1 pound medium shrimp, deveined and peeled

- 1 Tbsp. minced garlic

- 2 minced green onions

- 1 Tbsp. Minced cilantro

- 1 tbsp. hot sauce

- 1 Tbsp. favorite homemade spicy mustard

- 2 tbsp. olive oil

- 1 Tbsp. sesame seeds

Servings: 4

Preparation time: 30 min

Method:

You should use your largest skillet for this recipe or a wok.

Heat olive oil and cook the sesame seeds, green onions, cilantro with the garlic for about 7-8 minutes.

Add the shrimp, seasonings, hot sauce, mustard and lime juice.

Cook another 12-15 minutes or until the shrimp are done, turn pink.

Serve these spicy delicious shrimp on a salad, rice, or couscous.

Pizza with pickles and mustard

Pizzas are almost like canvas; they can be decorated just about with anything. You are creating your own masterpiece, and you should do it with pride. That's why when I serve this totally made-up pizzas to friends or neighbors, they are certainly congratulating me for my originality! I often propose my guess a dipping sauce made with mustard and sour cream, now that is a brave move, I dare you!

Ingredients:

- 1 large pizza crust

- ¼ pound ground beef

- 1 cup shredded American cheese

- ¼ cup dill pickles

- 1 tbsp. yellow mustard

- 1 Tbsp. olive oil

- 1 Tbsp. minced garlic

- Salt, black pepper

- 1 tsp. red pepper flakes

Servings: 4

Preparation time: 45 min

Method:

Preheat the oven to 400 degrees F.

Grease a pizza pan and set aside.

Place the crust on the pizza and line up all other ingredients on the kitchen counter.

In a medium pan, cook the ground beef with the mustard, and all seasonings.

Drain the fat well and set aside.

Brush olive oil and garlic on the pizza.

Spread the meat all over and then garnish with the pickles and top it off with the cheese.

Place in the oven for 30 minutes.

Serve of slice of this delicious pizza with a cold soda or a cold beer!

Roast beef and mustard wrap sandwiches

This recipe is not hard! It does not mean that it is not yummy, don't get me wrong! Wrap all the goodness in your favorite type of wrap. I enjoy using either spinach ones or sundried tomatoes, for the vivacious colors, I bring to the wrap.

Ingredients:

- 4 medium wheat, spinach or other types of tortilla breads

- 8 slices deli meat roast beef

- 1 Tbsp. favorite honey mustard

- 1 tbsp. mayonnaise

- Salt, black pepper

- 1 cup shredded iceberg lettuce

- 4 slices Swiss cheese

Servings: 4

Preparation time: 10 min

Method:

Heat the butter in a skillet and start cooking the onion. Add the vinegar and the honey after about 15 minutes and cook for an additional 5 minutes.

Green beans with mustard sauce

If you are a green bean's family like mine, you will also thrive on finding new recipes to serve these veggies. We love green beans, and we talk about green beans and dream about green beans quite often. So, when I presented this creation to my loved ones, they wanted green beans almost every day for a while week! This time, I am adding yellow beans for more colors!

Ingredients:

- 1 pound fresh trimmed green beans

- 1 pound fresh trimmed yellow beans

- 1 cup cooked and crumbled bacon bites

- 4 large hardboiled eggs, slices

- 2 Tbsp. minced red onion

- 1 Tbsp. lemon juice

- 1 Tbsp. Dijon mustard

- 1 tbsp. minced garlic

- 1 egg yolk

- Salt, black pepper

Servings: 4

Preparation time: 30 min

Method:

Wash and trim all the green and yellow beans.

Place them in a streamer over boiling water and steam cook the green beans for about 10 minutes.

Place them in a serving plate next.

In a small bowl, combine the lemon juice, mustard, garlic, egg yolk and seasonings.

Pour on the beans and stir so all get covered.

Slice hardboiled eggs and prepare crumbled bacon.

Add on top of the beans and place the serving plate in the middle of the table for everyone to help themselves.

Lovely honey and mustard baked ham

We are concluding this lovely cookbook with a big bang! This ham will blow you away. It mixes some of the most perfect ingredients And flavors for you to keep eating it until you hit the center bone! You will also love serving some leftover ham.

Ingredients:

- 1 X 5-6 pounds ham
- 1 Tbsp. yellow mustard
- 1 tbsp. spicy favorite homemade mustard
- 2 Tbsp. honey
- ¼ tsp. all spices
- ¼ tsp. nutmeg
- ¼ tsp. cinnamon
- 1 cup pineapple juice
- 1 tsp. red pepper flakes

Servings: 6-8

Preparation time: Several hours

Method:

Preheat oven to 350 degrees F.

Get a large aluminum pan or one of these disposable one too.

The rule of thumb is about 20 minutes per pound so if you have a 6 pounds ham, then 240 minutes so about 4 hours.

The trick is to always make sure your ham stays moist; no one wants to eat a dry ham!

Place your ham in the pan of your choice.

In a small saucepan, boil the pineapple juice, mustard, honey and all other ingredients.

Reduce temperature once it starts to thicken.

This mixture will become your glaze for the ham.

Use a cooking brush to spread all over the ham and place in the oven.

Keep any remaining of the sauce and some pineapple juice close by.

Set your timer every hour to check on the ham and keep it moist by pouring a little juice if needed.

After 2.5 hours or so of cooking time, you might want to cover it with aluminum foil. It depends how well roasted you like it.

Finish the cooking time. Cut the ham and test an area before serving to your loved ones.

Serve with mashed potatoes or other favorite sides.

Conclusion

There are so many things about mustard you do not know; we do feel like it's our duty to inform you and share additional interesting and fun facts. Therefore, here we go:

While you might think its ketchup, apparently mustard is the very first condiment people use. That is right, Egyptians actually buried the pharaohs in their tombs with mustard seeds: not the happiest way to use condiment, but very real and interesting. Then, Romans are the ones who started using the mustard seeds in the kitchen and mix it to create sauces or dishes.

Some health properties of the mustard seeds are amazing and should be known. For many centuries, the mustard seeds have been used to help with sinus issues, toothaches, appetite suppressants, asthmas relief, and immunity booster. Take a seed or tow!

Dijon mustard is not always from Dijon, do not be fooled! That's definitely where the name originated because of some additional ingredient that was added to the original recipe. Now, you can buy that name that product everywhere around the world.

Canada and Nepal are the countries that are producing the most mustard in the world.

If you are growing mustard and crushing the seeds hoping to get that very bright yellow you can find in the bottle, you might be slightly disappointed. That's because the yellow mustard we buy in the store has a touch of turmeric in it.

How long can you keep mustard? Almost forever! Seriously, if the mustard looks and taste fine, it is probably fine. Look at the expiration date, of course, but mostly the color and the overall look.

There is a Mustard museum in the state of Wisconsin. It displays over 5000 jars of mustard from around the work!

The average US citizen consumes about 12 ounces of mustard per year.

Is Mustard nutritious? Check this out: one teaspoon has less than 20 calories, no sugar, not fat, and about 5 mg of sodium. So, although it does not contain many nutrients, it does not contain any time to throw off your diet.

So now, you know almost everything on mustard, get ready to use it often, and have fun exploring many types of mustard in the kitchen. Impress your family and friends and bring them your own homemade spicy or sweet mustard that you made in a cute jar next time you visit!

About the Author

Ivy's mission is to share her recipes with the world. Even though she is not a professional cook she has always had that flair toward cooking. Her hands create magic. She can make even the simplest recipe tastes superb. Everyone who has tried her food has astounding their compliments was what made her think about writing recipes.

She wanted everyone to have a taste of her creations aside from close family and friends. So, deciding to write recipes was her winning decision. She isn't interested in popularity, but how many people have her recipes reached and touched people. Each recipe in her cookbooks is special and has a special meaning in her life. This means that each recipe is created with attention and love. Every ingredient carefully picked, every combination tried and tested.

Her mission started on her birthday about 9 years ago, when her guests couldn't stop prizing the food on the table. The next thing she did was organizing an event where chefs from restaurants were tasting her recipes. This event gave her the courage to start spreading her recipes.

She has written many cookbooks and she is still working on more. There is no end in the art of cooking; all you need is inspiration, love, and dedication.

Author's Afterthoughts

I am thankful for downloading this book and taking the time to read it. I know that you have learned a lot and you had a great time reading it. Writing books is the best way to share the skills I have with your and the best tips too.

I know that there are many books and choosing my book is amazing. I am thankful that you stopped and took time to decide. You made a great decision and I am sure that you enjoyed it.

I will be even happier if you provide honest feedback about my book. Feedbacks helped by growing and they still do. They help me to choose better content and new ideas. So, maybe your feedback can trigger an idea for my next book.

Thank you again

Sincerely

Ivy Hope

Made in United States
North Haven, CT
20 April 2022